Poems written from the heart

AF624526

Jamie Binkley

BookLeaf Publishing

Presentation by *BookLeaf Publishing*

Web: www.bookleafpub.com

E-mail: info@bookleafpub.com

ISBN: 9789357442961

First edition 2023

I am dedicating this book to those who are addicts homeless dealing with heartbreak depression anxiety basically to anyone who needs to hear them that it can inspire who ever his heart it may touch. The short book of poems is kind of like a short story of my life everyone has a story that needs to be read or heard and I hope this inspires those to write their story cuz someone's story can help another overcome the battles that they are battling so they can remember not to give up not to lose their face to believe in themself cuz anybody can be who they want to be and anybody can do what they want they just got to believe and have faith

A love turned into hate

My love for you want so strong your words are held on to so long but now I'm filled with so much hate your lies have sealed Our Fate my trust for you now is all gone your heart I thought was made of stone the love I had for you so deep has now turned into a bitter weep

A decision I regret

My heart was so naive so I never did believe that
you would be a mistake once I'd later have to
shake your lies and deceit left me feeling so beat
and now all I know I should have seen that you
were a decision I regret you I wish I had never
met

Strongest woman I know

Jennifer so strong and brave a warrior in her
own right her courage knows no bounds her
spirit swords with might her faith is unshakable
her heart is so full of love her will is
unbreakable she is a gift from the heavens above
she is my niece one that I surely love

Second Chances

Life's not a game Second Chances are rare a second chance is a chance to repair what we've done wrong what we've said amiss a chance to write our wrongs and take a different path a second chance is a chance to forgive a chance to try again a chance to live a chance to show our strength to show we care and chance for a fresh start a second chance to share

Beautifully Broken

Beautifully Broken yet still alive fragile and weary yet still strive no longer perfect but still Divine Darkness and Light a perfect entwine lost and confused yet still remain Clinging On to Hope despite the pain I saw that's been shattered yet still stands tall a heart that's been broken yet still loves all. This is part of my story part of who I am today,I hope it reaches out and touches you all. Despite the pain that still remains I'm standing strong again with Shields to block my fall

Real or fake

A man of fake a man of real both have a story they can tell one is a lie one is true which one is which no one knew a mask of the seat a heart of gold one is a mystery one is bold a man of Truth a man of Lies both have a place in our lives but we figure out which one it's fake and tells all the lies we were part of our ways without any goodbyes

A true friend

A true friend is like a bouquet bright fresh and full of grace a shoulder to lean on a light and life's darkest place a voice to hear my stories a heart to feel my pain a smile to share my Joys loyalty that will remain

In my addiction I once was

A slave to the craving and lust my life was a mess and they fuss I was lost in my own distrust broken and filled with Dread my future seems so Sleek my will was gone my heart was dead I was drowning in my own bleak stable environments good people and sobriety I will always seek

Closure

The path is winding the road is long the journey
is hard the way is strong the pain of the past that
hurt is deep the future is uncertain fears I keep
the closure I seek the healing I need the courage
to face the wounds to bleed the hope of
Tomorrow the day of more than the peace that
comes when I am Reborn

A blessing scent

A blessing Sent From Heaven above a gift of Grace and love to fill my heart with joy and peace and bring me hope that will not cease I'd like to guide me through the night the street to help me put up the fight a promise of joy that will never end a blessing sent to be my friend that blessing I hope will never end

Time for change

Time is the essence of life changes a must to survive being a day a month or a year let us break old habits and steer to A New Path a different goal let us take the chance and roll away from the status quo towards a brighter future we go with change better days are coming this we do know

A marriage failed

Two hearts that wants be in time now drift apart
and life's design life's promise is so hard to keep
loves hopes and dreams now take a leap two
people who wants to give out now find that trust
and faith have flown no more laughter no more
Smiles the marriage failed a broken mile

Narcissist

A creature So Vain a monster of pride a creature of self with a swollen ego inside a soul so consumed they fail to become the one they love is their self-defined the world around them is only their stage it's their own image that they must engage to wrapped up in themselves to see others needs a narcissist life is a sorrowful deed they will definitely make our hearts bleed

Angel from above

A friend was sent to me he was a great source of support during difficult times he would always listen to me talk about my worries and gave me valuable advice and did all he could to lend a hand on all my needs he's always there for me no matter what I was going through he's empathetic understanding and patient and he always has my best interest in mind he is an invaluable source of comfort and strength during tough times he was like a lighthouse in a storm providing a Beacon of Hope in the midst of dark and turbulances his presence is truly a blessing and he will always remain in my heart and memories cuz a friend who always will be the angel sent from above to guide me.

Peace and quiet

Star shining so bright you want to get lost in the night silence except sounds of nature it's a piece that kind of want to save her our future is bright we try with all of our might Keeping the Faith knowing we're not going to lose this fight our scars reminds us of all the pain and restraints that bounded us since then we haven't been the same we all have fought tooth in there even come back up from the depths of Hell to remain sane friends and family do not worry we all have a story one day it will be hurt or written people didn't listen when that day comes then we will have our Glory

Till I see you again

Sitting all alone in my room always feeling so Gloom mind racing trouble sleeping thinking of nothing except you is it true are we really through I'm clueless I need a reason I truly want to know why God Made You just the season thanks we have said are done to each other could it ever just be forgiven and you I had a friend that I wish I could mend why does this have to be our end I hope that one day maybe on different terms we do meet again so safe travel until then my friend I do hope we meet again

Lost

He brought me out of the dark into the light I still see you in my dreams at night I had your trust from the start what happened to your heart my love I thought we'd always be together and never be apart when I thought of you I felt love now all I feel is a lot of hate that I do not want in my heart it is going to break my faith I wish it all would just fade away it's killing What's Left of Me. Still today I have love for you all I can do is pray all these bad days will pass and go away. Was your love ever real or true,you forgot about me,today I still think of only you.

My dog in heaven

Lucky the time we had together I sure wish it would have lasted forever now that you're gone sometimes I miss you so much I feel sad and all alone a gift I got that's a part of you he keeps me from feeling so blue especially when I'm thinking of you I call him Papa but lucky junior is his name he looks and reminds me of you so much it's insane but in my heart you will always remain

Wasted time

Bad choices Wasted Years it was like walking down a dark hallway with no end in sight I was constantly making the wrong turns and had to struggle to find my way back after much reflection I finally came to the realization that I had to make better decisions in order to make move forward and leave the dark hallway behind by understanding I had to make better choices I was able to exit the dark hallway of Wasted Years and start doing a brighter path it took me some time to understand that I had the power to make positive changes in my life I had to be willing to try different things and not be afraid to make mistakes once I started to focus on making better decisions and taking positive actions I was able to take control of my life and put myself on a path I knew was right.

Addiction

I am an addict that I will always be but that doesn't Define who I am or God's purpose for me. And I struggle with addiction but it doesn't stop me from being the person I am meant to be for example I put my energy into helping others overcome the same struggles I have endured and this is how I Define my purpose in life it's like I'm a butterfly with a broken wing determined to fly anyway I may be stuck in some of my bad habits but that doesn't mean I am not capable of soaring I believe everyone has the power to make a difference in the world regardless of their circumstances I'm using my experiences to try to make a positive impact to be an example of how you can still make a difference even if you are dealing with addiction I'm taking my broken wing and I'm using it to propel me a direction that will help others

After the storm

Same light after the darkness can be a sign of Hope and a reminder that even the darkest times can come to an end it can signify A New Beginning a time for healing and growth and a time for us to move forward and Men it is like a rainbow after a storm giving us a moment of beauty and respite after the chaos of the rain and wind it gives us something to look forward to a reminder that Friday so what are we waiting for let our journey begin and fight to win

www.ingramcontent.com/pod-product-compliance
Lightning Source LLC
Chambersburg PA
CBHW051721130826
49812CB00034B/1296
* 9 7 8 9 3 5 7 4 4 2 9 6 1 *